Days of Destruction

by

Gary Beck

ISBN: 978-81-19228-52-2

First Edition: 2023
Rs. 200/-

Cyberwit.net
HIG 45 Kaushambi Kunj, Kalindipuram
Allahabad - 211011 (U.P.) India
http://www.cyberwit.net
Tel: +(91) 9415091004
E-mail: info@cyberwit.net

To Nancy, Whose charm, grace, wit and artistry enrich my life.

Some of these poems have appeared in:

Aim Magazine, San Francisco Poetry Journal, First Class Magazine, Kota Press, Clark Street Review, Nuvein Magazine, Down In the Dirt Magazine, New Verse News, Ya' Sou!, Poetic Voices, The November 3rd Club Journal, The Neovictorian/Cochlea, Enigma, The Argotist Online, AIA Poetry, Poetry Midwest, Pegasus Magazine, KuPoZine, Flutter Magazine, Lost Owl Poetry, Existenz,

Contents

Prisons

Let them enter into your gates
for comfort from the new mother,
and father who won't abandon
the lost boys and girls, playing cool,
acting tough, trying to conceal
the desperate loss of hope, the fear
that they may be without value,
to the world that's based on profit.

The winds from Washington D.C.
are blowing in state capitals,
and funneled to the big cities,
where citizens of confusion,
disciples of the lottery,
are conditioned to evasion
of thankless chores to do what's right
that never seem to earn rewards.

Across this land of bitterness,
divided by have nots and haves,
a growing sense of failure cries
to lock kids up, or shoot them down.
A democratic decision
that was made without much wisdom
to let kids kill each other off
and put survivors behind bars.

The gates of welcome opened wide
for victims of our kind neglect,

the kids we chose to throw away
because it costs too much to care.
What sins we make them suffer for,
these babies born to stand alone.
What price they pay to learn their crimes,
offspring from schools of violence.

The citizens of our country
demand more prisons for our kids.
Fund them, build them, staff them, run them,
then everyone will make money.
For those who dream philosophy
we'll teach them true economics:
there's no profit in prevention,
nor in rehabilitation.

It matters not how bad the drugs
that leave kids lifeless in the streets,
as long as dealers make their loot
and neighbors help them ply their trade.
We close our eyes to all the needs
that don't put cash in our pockets
and the harm that's done to our youth
doesn't count to politicians,
because kids don't vote.

Endangered

Born to diminishing flocks,
I can no longer find
the nest of my fathers.
In the third year since hatching,
I wearily dance the courtship dance,
I hoarsely cry the mating call,
but no one answers.
I hardly remember
my nestling time
when the chirps of my mother,
alert for marauders,
warned me of danger.
Now the predators are departed,
dispersed by man the protector,
guardian of my growing fear,
that I will never sing the marriage song.

Manhattan Lodging

Midtown welfare hotel
with rooms of residential hell.
Mother does her business on the bed.
Bro shoots heroin until he's dead.
Little bro breaks into telephones.
Sis studies mom and doesn't miss a trick.
When the dealers don't hang out in front
tourists sometimes enter by mistake
looking for that elusive bargain,
convenient midtown hotel.

Sliding to Tomorrow

I walk down rubbled streets,
Beirut, Bombay, and Baghdad,
hated by young and old,
Black, White, Hispanic, poor,
alike in resentment
for my brief visit
to the museum of squalor,
a display of suffering,
an exhibition of shame,
a show that will continue
until spectation ends.
But then I suddenly realize
this is not a third world nightmare,
we're in America,
declining to decay,
since no one knows enough
to stop the fall.

Lost Children

Far from the halls of learning
our criminal children stray
committing their violent deeds
in a younger, more vicious way.
Far from a parent's guidance
our bewildered offspring roam
confused, frightened, resentful,
convinced that they stand alone.
Far from the comfort of churches,
they could not find an open door,
or what's normal now in cities,
the priest couldn't help them anymore.
Now lost to the comforts of home,
abandoned by their family,
they huddle in prisons or shelters,
convicted, condemned to poverty.

The Conquest of Somalia

Mogadishu, Mogadishu,
you have almost been forgotten
by our leaders who sent soldiers
(seeking glorious victories)
to patrol your poor, dusty streets
and tremble in the rains of evening
from tropical disease, or fear,
dazed by one more unclear mission,
dumped on our obedient troops,
ordered to build a quick triumph,
so D.C. strutters and prancers
could boast their boasts and brag their brags
that the administration kicked ass.

We saw action, Mogadishu,
but once again we sailed away
on sullen ships that knew defeat.
Movers and fixers surrendered
(they always do when things get tough)
'cause they didn't know how to capture
the gangster, tyrant, war-lord, thug,
the uncooperative foe
who would not let the boys and girls
of Washington, D.C. look good.

So we landed on your beaches
crammed with the waiting media
equipped with cameras, mikes, lights,
greeting our surprise invasion.

We couldn't turn back with CNN
directing us to storm ashore,
their instant satellite transmission
displaying the troop's deployment
(that only took six weeks longer
then the troops in the Crimean War)
to a hundred million viewers
watching our embarrassed leaders,
caught once again with their plans down,
who chose to sacrifice the lives
of G.I.'s who followed orders,
rather than admit they were wrong.
So the troops were ordered ashore,
fought off media resistance
(refusing to land one more time
to give viewers better footage)
and took minimal casualties
from the international press.
We marched without the faintest clue
where the hell Mogadishu was,
but we lucked out, for CNN
cut to its commercial break
and missed our heroic capture
of the Somalia dispatcher
of the local cab company,
who not only took the short cut,
but charged us out of season rates.

Every foreign correspondent,
even the cub from the Tribune,
and one hundred million viewers,
through the courtesy of CNN,
knew the expedition arrived.

But there wasn't a single link
on the rusty chain of command
with common sense enough to say:
"I'm sorry, sir. They know we're here."
Even general whats-his-name
who we were supposed to arrest
(or was it bomb, or execute?
The orders never were quite clear.)
had concessionaires on the beach,
selling souvenirs to the troops.
But we couldn't billet the soldiers
in beautiful beachfront hotels
(even though it's out of season
and they offered us tourist rates)
without orders from higher up.

Traditional rooters who loved
frequent failures of the U.S. of A.
chuckled from hooches, tents, shanties,
snickering at our willing troops
marching to a police action,
pursued by hordes of at-risk youth
demanding the usual pay,
the American subsidies,
gum, chocolate, cigarettes, and coke,
promising in return their best wares
shoe shines, virgin sisters, great dope,
the usual native exchange.

Now warrior Bill took D.C.
just promoted from C.I.C.
of the Arkansas National Guard,
ready for foreign adventure,

grasped the big picture at a glance,
inflated for authority,
reddened with exasperation,
glistened with anticipation
gained from motel campaigns
at the head of his state troopers,
bellowed with combat assurance
to the combined wisdom of D.C.,
"What the hell do we do now, huh?"
Both Sonorous and Clamorous
orated at length from the floor
and Sonorous requested peace,
but Clamorous demanded war.

So Bill and Hil went up the hill
to fetch some help from Congress.
But Bill fell down and broke his crown
and Hil came tumbling after....

There we were deployed for battle,
with tribesmen to the left of us,
and tribesmen to the right of us,
and the U.N. all around us.
CNN reporters were poised
to describe to the world our advance
along the Boulevard of Broken Dreams,
as we entered a new city
that sure wasn't American,
so all the destruction was foreign.
Now that doesn't mean we believe
that underdeveloped nations
need extensive devastation
before getting reconstruction,

but if you want us to rebuild,
we first have to blow everything up.

(With diverse methodologies
that assault with technologies.
The selection is enormous,
without long lines, or other fuss)

We offer smart bombs, laser bombs,
A-bombs, H-bombs, cluster bombs,
fragmentation bombs, broadway bombs,
racial discrimination bombs,
mortar bombs and pestle bombs,
even ultimate doomsday bombs.
There are bombs that make you happy,
" " " " " " wheeze,
" " " " " " grouchy,
" " " " " " sneeze....
There is nothing quite like a bomb.
Nothing that can compare with it.
Nothing that even competes with it.
Its explosion is detonous.

So we were tortured by tse-tse's,
mutilated by mosquitos,
made delirious with desire,
polluted and prostituted,
then we were driven mad by you,
our treacherous Mogadishu.

Time Past

Long before complex social spectators
informed the slower of our citizenry
that wealth was distributed unequally,
envious early man sulked in the cave
when he didn't receive a fair share
of recently acquired meat, fat, fur.

Who Careth For....

I have seen so many children,
heirs to the American dream,
suffering in our prisons.
It must be my fault.
After all, somebody caused those kids,
the lost bodies of poverty
to miss the lessons that prevented
the violent commission of
murder, arson, robbery, rape,
before the tender age of twelve.
I have sat with them
behind medium or very secure doors
that keep them locked away,
far from the hope of our poor memory,
removed from our responsibility.
Yet somebody caused these kids
to trespass beyond forgiveness.
You swear it wasn't you,
but it had to be someone.
All those kids didn't get up one morning
and suddenly commit horrible crimes.
So it must be me,
'cause if it wasn't you....

Arms Race

Stealth technology
will make a mockery
of crime detection
and civil insurrection.

Stealth tanks
muffle clanks.

Smart bombs
end calms.

Anti-missile missiles
seldom send epistles.

Helicopter gunships
give foes fat lips.

Laser aiming
is quite maiming.

G.I. Joe
till don't know.

Bag Lady

No longer young,
but not much older than me,
I have seen her often
in subway visions,
ravaged by her treasure
simmering in shopping bags,
her eyes the hunger of zoo animals,
with a wrinkled, worried face
that will not allow tomorrows.

Parade Rest

After the battle is over
the soldiers return to their barracks
and we organize a homecoming parade
that costs millions of dollars
to greet our splendid warriors,
who did their job properly
and killed our enemies.
Then there are our leaders
who boldly snatched billions
and sent our armies abroad
and enforced economic sanctions
in tiny, totalitarian kingdoms,
while millions of our people
petitioned our government in vain
for desperately needed assistance.
Instead of expensively presenting
the legions in their splendour,
we should have an honor guard
for each branch of the service
proudly bear the flag up Broadway,
slogging through the tickertape
to our cheers and gratitude,
and we'll use the money saved
in judicious investments
for the future of our children.

This Good Life

What is the hunger of water-falls
for little men in tiny boats,
flirting with alluring whirlpools,
who lie on crowded Sunday beaches
dreaming of vacations in the winter,
burdened by cameras that seek
Palm Beach condos,
Fort Lauderdale motels,
Miami hotels.
The tourists sleep late, swim,
drive on across an aging land,
veined with highways of destruction,
submerged with cities of corrosion,
skeletoned by crumbling towns and farms,
and always arteries of roads, roads, roads,
coursing its people like blood
through a diseased body,
until one day
the price of oil
ends our way.

Hotel

It was late at night.
I was tired, dirty, hungry,
dissolving into salesman's squalor
after an unprofitable day.
My feet were as asleep as my mind
when the taxi turned the corner
onto a remembered midtown street
that suddenly looked slum at me.
Hostile black and latino families,
carelessly sprawled on the steps,
in undershirts, shorts, new sneakers,
beer cans dripping with resentment,
offered no welcome to a weary traveler.

I stumbled to the registration desk,
sample cases sagging to the ground,
besieged by unofficial bellhops
eager to relieve me of my burden.
The desk was guarded
by a plexiglass clerk
who refused to notice me.
I knocked until he responded,
requested a room with private bath,
was charged 50% more than last year,
and much too weary for dispute,
took the urine scented elevator
up past yells and curses,
to my dim, dank floor.

The room was shabby, smelly, sullen,
stained by the liquid history of occupants.
I was too exhausted to depart,
so I barricaded my door,
curled up in my clothes
on the over-experienced bed,
only stirring with apprehension
at the screams of sex and violence.

Morning did not come too soon.

I rinsed my face, combed my hair,
picked up my bags, went to the door,
rode the aromatic elevator
to the lobby of release.
I only paused to ask the clerk,
who looked as harsh as famine,
what changed things since last year.
As I went out the door of reprieve
he yelled that it had recently become
a hotel for the homeless.

Apres Moi....

Confusion is normal in our times,
declining security at home,
increasing menace from abroad.
Those above us are stingy
and refuse to sacrifice one meal.
Those below us are resentful,
as those below have always been,
but now are almost threatening
as the scum of Paris streets
to the carriaged aristocrats.
One of our recent presidents
mumbled about the deluge,
but neglected to order shipyards
to build vessels of survival.

Schism

As soon as the church forgot
how to keep the congregation hopping,
sin was no longer regularly combated
(the Sunday bouts have lost their luster)
and in the ever widening separation
between the spirit and the values,
the sermon of the electronic age
bombards us with the compelling particles,
subatomic impulses commanding
buy, consume, waste, want,
purchase repentance.

Moment of Memory

You are the penny candy
of wide-eyed children,
the bright red sour ball
of almost disremembered taste
of Lone Ranger, Green Hornet
Inner Sanctum ago.
Once you too had innocence,
but you have joined
the paunched men of sin,
in steamrooms of atonement,
where sweat runs down flaccid jowls,
escaping pitiful pink mouths
protesting the pain of awareness
that their guilt will be forgotten.

Closed Case

Hopes and dreams wait on the welfare lines,
faces masked by newspapers, books, facades,
apprehensive, but not caring about others.
The shoving bodies surge closer
to the desks of denial
that burden the tired, hungry, needy,
citizens and aliens alike
who no longer fear rejection flames
from purifying clerks
who cleanse the poor.

Rate of Return

Mothers are no longer sufficient
to deter criminal behavior
in the evolving absence of fathers.
It's easier to blame some one,
(or poverty, or race)
but it should be evident
that man the unruly animal
always requires nurturing,
and sooner or later
if he doesn't get it,
someone else will suffer for it.

Truce in Iraq

The invasion is over.
The last battle has ended
and our victorious forces have prevailed.
The fears of disaster have disappeared
and the clamors of protest are silent.
Those who were expected to perish
celebrated in their foxholes,
empty beercans piled higher
then the heap of the dead.
The shock of combat has faded.
Misgivings have departed faster
than changes in public opinion,
except the unpleasant question:
why did we spend so much,
to kill so many,
with such little concern,
when we're going to do it again?

Devolution

Somewhere in the South Florida habitat
migration became mostly human,
replacing birds, bees, beasts,
overwhelmed by hotels, motels, condos,
that swallowed a peninsular tract
once the showpiece of a continent,
that allowed coexistence of species
who were not permitted to vote,
were denied government protection,
were encouraged to disappear,
or beg on man made marinas,
another callous testimony
of progress to destruction.

Beggar

A derelict woman with tangled hair,
unkempt shirt, open pants, peeling skin,
stabs her hand through the night at me,
rattling a grimy paper cup,
urgently demanding money.
She refuses to sink into the pavement
and disrupts my prosperous transit
through this insecure world.
A glimpse of her unzipped flesh
beckons violent visions
of mindless sex, vicious rape.
Helpless to alter her destiny,
my lack of power
sends my hand to my pocket
seeking coins to oblivion.

Neglect

Too many Americans ignore the world of chaos
and forget the men who hold the buttons
that will ignite atomic weapons
that never stop longing for fission.
We sit in the comfort of home,
newspapered, TV'd and dreamy,
neglectful of our friends and foes,
while our poor children are banned
from the cornucopia of science
and will not discover
that the barns of rotting grain
on some distant government preserve
will never be theirs to savor.

Visit to the Past

I walked the lower east side street
where I once lived
poverty lifetimes ago.
The tired dirt still peeked
from children's faces,
although of different races.
I saw the window across the street
where once a naked harpist sat
and strummed midnight serenades.
The woman with seven cats
who hated me as much
as she hated my ferocious dog,
glared at me as if I'd never been away.
All the despised and dispossessed
are still imprisoned here,
enduring the all-consuming streets.

Warning to Seniors

Our parents are strangling our children,
throttling, choking, suffocating,
cutting off the breath of future life.
Arise offspring of prosperity
before they consume our posterity,
as they waste a generation's supplies
and pile their refuse to the skies.

After the great migration to the sun belt,
as thoughtless as the buffalo,
the grey heads, tired of service,
yearning for the condos of security,
destroying more and more of the land,
our dwindling forests and waterways,
for uniform retirement communities,
comfortable conclaves of the idle old.

There is no covenant
between man and nature
that allows our elders to decide
when to give up their responsibility
to the future of society.

In Another Land, Lost

In the Bahnhof waiting room,
too poor to buy a ticket,
awakened from kindly dreams
by the harsh hands of the police
pulling me off the slumber table,
shoving me out of the darkened restaurant,
mumbling, stumbling, tranced,
into the chill Dusseldorf night,
bowed by sagging shoulders,
dulled almost beyond continuation,
swaying, sniffling, drained of fervor,
only avoiding collapse
with the hope of warm refuge.

I am homeless this night,
my fears the same as others,
the arrival of tomorrows.
Where will we go,
o enemies of the morning?
Shall we meet again?
Perhaps tomorrow night,
heads couched on arms, dirtier,
owning only sad enchantments.
Shall I be the last inventor,
or have I more to surrender?
If I survive the perils of daylight,
I shall stay awake all evening,
blinking greetings at strangers,
rigid with protests and yearnings,

trapped in spittle and droolings,
tobaccoed and tarnished,
once again lifeless lumps
inert upon the tables,
trapped between sleep and death.

Ignored by all except authority
babbling to anyone who listens,
I see another homeless creature
cautiously stir and peer about,
gently shaking his tiny wife awake.
They look at each other.
I see you, stranger
a moment in this bitter life
and ebb away, drifting….Nowhere….

In the Bahnhof waiting room
I have become lost,
waiting for nothing.

Ages Past

Naishapur and Babylon
were once flowering cities
of innumerable splendors
that attracted barbarian hordes
eager to be temporary guests
of civilization's comforts.
After the visitors rode on,
never looking back at luxury,
the cities never bloomed again
and the traditional conflict
between dishonest townspeople
and destructive marauders,
continued to this very day.

Morning

The city stirs another day
with rumbles, shakes, groans and howls,
unsyncopated in its display.

Guided by a mad conductor,
without established structural sway
the orchestra of man, machine, streets,
performs its alien function
in an unharmonious way.

City song that drowns tomorrow
with echoes of a harsh incision
that amputates the dawn of sorrow
and leaves the last chant of derision.

The Decay of Cities

America, the proud and free
once the world's praises sang of thee.
Now as hated as Rome or Athens,
we have frayed the hope of liberty.

Cities past are really cities present,
or future, only different
in design, habit, custom
made by people past, for people present,
or future, only different
in size, shape, color.

Congested habitations
consistently jumble together
non-supportive groups
often in conflict,
or unfair competition
for diminishing resources

Tour Guide

Come with me
along the crumbling streets of cities
swallowing transient tenants
in devouring yawns,
leaving only hats and gloves behind.
We pause a moment
on congested corners,
strutting or slinking
to homes, to stores, to schools,
through hazardous parks,
not yet immune to danger.

Ruminations

O say can you see
how the bureaucracy
makes it harder and harder
to replenish the larder.

Coastal cities
consume the earth faster
than river cities,
though it's harder to notice

Declining species
punish their saviors
by not saying thank you
for being preserved.

Persecuted creatures
rarely have sufficient time
to prepare evolutionary defenses
against man the intruder,
who gets there fastest
with the worstest.

The more superficial our society
the more we fear variety.

There's safety in sameness,
which renders us blameless.

Evolution

Puzzle this creation,
things merge
breeding change,
come together,
part again
on a weak earth,
listless and sedate,
(an old prim ma'am,
eyeing a child's soiled fingers)
waiting for a man's departure.

Helplessness

A pale, molecular vision
possesses me, then moves away.
A dark, chemical apparition
visits me, but will not stay.
Confined to regrets,
my scientific mechanisms
refuse to obey.
I cannot cry for help,
confined to sullen silence
by an electronic display.

Control

In prosperous apartments
comfortable people dwell
manacled to microwaves,
riveted to vcrs,
spreadeagled on stereos,
trapped in electronic submissions
that provide delight
and erase public concern
with remote control.

Oppression

Studio of unknown signals,
historical messages,
illusions of alien folk
with incomprehensible tools,
enamoured of incessant clamour,
besieging us with video visions,
wonders from a spectacle of blight.
We no longer sing enough,
trapped in limited vistas,
anguished by hopes of incandescence,
guided by artificial masters
consuming our intelligence.

This Message is....

Sociological phenomenon
attract more attention
when registering information
on the public awareness
when presented by our friends, the media.
Nothing makes us better understand
crime, poverty, disease, drugs,
the moral aberrations
that destroy the social fabric
with violent conclusions,
that never seem to result in
revolutionary change.

Conditioning

Facts are more consoling,
whether right or wrong,
than uncertain speculations.
We prefer to lurch and stumble blindly,
caught in the age of electronic enlightenment
that breeds chemical acceptance
without clinical comfort.

Empire

We stood upon the shores of ruin
and watched the risk laden ships
boldly sail the masterless seas
and trembled, remembering the plenty,
the promise of Pax Americana
with the entire world a grip away
as we sagely waited to snatch
future victory from present defeat
and avoided that flex of strength
that always alarms a narrowed world.

Isolated Armies

Morning mist
rises from Valley Forge,
obscuring history.
Cars rush past me
as I stand thumb extended,
waiting for a ride west.
I vision colonial soldiers
of long ago endurance,
staining the snow with bloody footprints.
I remember their struggles,
cold, tired, hungry, frightened,
abandoned by Congress,
as so many of our armies
have been abandoned by Congress,
as they sacrificed for others.
Ancient ghosts dissolve
into the consuming fog of time past
and a distant drum taps tomorrows.
A car stops. I get in. We drive away.
Behind us dwindles consecration.

Tarawa

I think of bloody Tarawa,
a wasteful battle of blunders
where the juice of youth dyed the sea,
the bombs brutalized the shore,
the processional of the dead,
ours and theirs inseparable
in an obscuring history
that obliterated cause and claim,
leaving a littered atoll,
hosting dank, decaying jungle
forever concealing a bitter fight
on land, sea, air, for old men's whim,
paid with patriotic soldier's pain
that now is almost forgotten.
Historical Fact

People once built thick walls
around prosperous cities
to keep wealth in, undesirables out.
Gunpowder convinced city planners
to abandon false hopes
for a secure future
and build better streets
for the convenience of invaders,
so they wouldn't resent delays
getting to the center of town
for easier pillage and looting.

Urban Wall

I visited a small Swiss town
neat, orderly, clean,
isolated from the change of time.
Folk still live in the massive wall
that once kept enemies outside,
and is as secure today
as life ever gets
for poor folk in Switzerland,
or anywhere else.

California Vision

As I walked the coast road
the morning mist covered unexpected valleys,
then a sudden unveiling of secret places
revealed treasures almost beyond enduring;
green slopes, dotted with cattle,
strayed from Texas to route 1 mountain crannies
that grazed near the surfer's ocean,
while I hummed get along little doggie
to self-conscious California cowboys
thinking of their surf boards,
and a distant beach,
with giant breakers
slightly out of reach.

For Want Of

The boundary lines are clearly drawn.
The well-to-do have fortified
their unassailable positions,
determined to repulse at all costs
the incursions of the needy.
Diminishing resources require
careful conservation, a good plan
to resist demands for equal sharing.
Division by need won't work.
The soviet collapse,
fracturing to ethnic rivalries,
is more than convincing proof
for us to seek a better way
for consensual consideration.

We Interrupt....

Many mistakes allow correction,
wounded human feelings top the list,
but accidents that cause catastrophe,
car crash, train collision, airplane down,
leave little leeway for apology,
since numerous fatalities
often disturb tranquility
and hurts relatives and friends,
who never find consolation
in stories on the evening news.

Distant Hopes

Spinner of resplendent dreams
who offers nights of opulence,
you stir elements of evil,
laziness and lust,
two leering gargoyles
riding opiated madmen
on the camel of forgetfulness,
mocking with taloned fingers
the search for Himalayan visions.
We laugh....Sing....Shout....
O dazed weaver
spinning your credulous thread,
there is just one lost drum,
relentlessly beating in the night.

Frail Visions

And the people went out of their houses
and stood together in the night,
and a great star flickered in the night,
and a dazzling light covered the land,
and peace was born.
And men no longer went out
to slay their neighbors,
and women no longer were lonely,
and children no longer were afraid.
But the night passed
and I awakened from delusion
and the day turned bright
and burned away my foolish dream.

Easy Dreaming

The little boy
of no home,
torn clothes,
school's done,
lost hopes,
supports the Congress
of this here United States
by hanging out,
instead of learning.

Fancy Judas

Old man of no legs
longing for the automat,
sensitive as Cyrano
tired of callous prying
at his insensate mutters.
His last supper tray,
piled with meager fare
and sad blessings,
drops thirty slices of toast,
accusing us
of irreverence and impiety.
Defenseless,
we dodge the plumes of drool
and watch him waft away,
industrious as death.

Lost Dog

Cry in the distance,
I forgot, I forgot,
all the acts and deeds
that I have done.
Will night come again?
A little dog lifts his leg,
pees on the last tree,
winks at me,
stretching his infinite leash,
belly full of laughs and belches
and barks farewell
to a kindless master.

Flight

Running madly,
like a mad king to his palace
trembling from the brutal roar
of hungry cannibals,
through the howling streets
past cobra children,
hyena men,
leopard women,
until he cowers in
the safety of the zoo.

I am 27

I grasp the world of promise,
a hungry Goth or Vandal
battering on Roman doors.
I am soothed by pledges.
I pause assaults
expecting triumphs,
lusting the changes
from shabby cloth
to splendid garment.
Then the voices of betrayal
whisper in deceptions
and drive me to migrations.

I am Thirty

Surrounded by the ripped visions
of my futile dreaming
and the fading intensities
that lingered for a few hungers
and no longer crave glory,
but before my embalming,
endures the hope for completion,
Poetmen, I still may join you.

Rock Star

After our feeling for the rock star fades,
where do they go when they are forgotten?
The strumming, stomping, smashed guitars,
the sweat, hot lights, torn clothes
are finally ended.
After that there is no message.

Treaty

Your fingers, diplomats,
divide my desire,
and race across my body
recognizing no borders.
Unharmed and helpless
I watch your armies
feast on my flesh.
Your volcano mouth,
blinding as a star's birth,
erupts my vision
and your perfume of invasion
compels my surrender.

Meeting

Your eyes lingered on me
devouring my substance, heat
imagined flew between us
baring our senses, kind
hunger relented one lazy moment
long enough.
I touched your urchin arm.

You followed 'til we reached my room
unchastening my need, gifts
weakening me in anticipation
dazing me childlike, blind
denying any me screaming
for protection.
I shed your soft garments

You met me a hot sun of morning
falling on a dry field, fierce
motions storming two barren bits
crazed with plenty's promise, fury
spilling out, raging us locked
choiceless.
I sang our wild passion.

You fell from me still silent
shaking from release, past
anguishes of disappointment, raising

a remorseless serpent jealous, lost
the indescribable selection
refuge.
You fled my loveless room.

Amaryllis

Voluptuous blossom that could consume
all our lust for beauty with one bloom
that unfolds for a brief sharing,
in natures sexual surrender to man
with exquisite delight, compelling attention,
quickly reaching the delectable climax,
swiftly dwindling to brown, fallen petals,
an ache of remembrance, a gift departed.

Disconnected

I lost my love in a telephone booth
in a drugstore on Broadway.
It cost 25 cents.
I lost my precious gift
of time, joy,
her teeth fastened to my neck.
I heard her voice, remote,
speaking in another tongue
that I could not understand.
I screamed my anguish,
love, need,
I want to nibble on your ear lobe.
She could not hear me.
A rancorous operator translated:
"I'll call you if I change my mind."
I stood at the counter,
paid for an aspirin heart
and went home
to listen for the telephone.

Resistance

People of my generation,
so quick to listen
to each deceit from thwarted men,
we truly are the heirs of puny sires.
Our age may overwhelm us with confusion,
but we are the children of destruction,
who cry: What shall we do?
Show us a direction,
when we should slay the past
in ruthless insurrection
against torpid elders,
who yearn for moderation.
We must demand impetuous change,
until we can reveal ourselves
as youthful revolutionaries,
storming an oppressive Bastille
and stir old men with clamoring commotion
that converts their idle sleep to motion.

To Baudelaire

Wraithing a world
of opiate lusts
and crazed virtues,
you dreamed that boredom
sucked upon his hookah,
potent and eternal.

Smug rests imperfection,
supine on silk cushions,
eyes bulging with amusement
as the human creation
bursting with revelation,
cries to ascend.

Ruler

The tyrant has many servants,
runs on eager legs for power
and is determined and awful.
The empty bellies of children
do not disturb him.
He will never be merciful
and will not let us defy him,
so we must be cautious
in the elevation
of elected leaders.

Hot Times

Brush fire blazing,
rushing faster
than swollen rivers,
banks open for business,
staffed by waiting crocodiles
watching from lazy lizard eyes,
the mad monkey pack
scurrying through tree tops,
unaware of predators
following on unctuous legs,
more patient than prophets
eager to do business.

Odium

I am weary of the constant thoughts of love
tumbling like cranky acrobats
from an unplugged porcelain jug.
My mind is reeling
from the blasting sound of you,
insistent as a stale bassoon.
I walk the confines of my coffin room
without the cemetery weight of memories
ripping through the cracked and rotting walls
of my retention of you,
with the merciless precision
of a carnal typhoon.

Random Thoughts

Pride is the crutch
on which failures rest.

We sleep, yet rest not,
consumed by nuclear dreams.

We are old wars
waiting to happen.

We are trapped on the beaches of Elba
awaiting a favorable sign.

We have forgotten the nights
when flesh would fall together,
splashing higher than destruction.

The Temple of Sin

"Once upon this very spot,"
said the old one to the young,
"a thousand pearls of nature bloomed.
The sprites and elves in beauty decked
sought out the dew on summer morns
and drank the earthly crystal drops.
The birds attired in rainbow doublets
sang of radiant liberty
and trees and bushes heard the song
and joined in gleeful dance.
Throughout the field stillness reigned
and serenity prevailed,
until the gruff-voiced workmen came
and felled the trees and crushed the flowers.
Then did all their beasts of prey,
the roaring metal monsters,
disembowel the battered field
with a soulless monument to man.
So progress came," the old one said
to the inattentive young.
The field is gone,
its dwellers banished or destroyed.
Just the birds remain.
Perched upon this modern temple tall
they sing in sad lament of beauties past,
but, who listens to the birds?

And Guide Us....

God bless Americ
a land of plent
your house may not be ful
love your neighborhoo
despite the hate and strif
enabling others to cry sham
essences pass as stiff as childre
never pausing to play game
so god bless Americ
a happy plac
e.

Dwindling Nests

The bird of summer has flown south,
winging farewell to colder clime.
Arrival is uncertain,
since endless hazards,
natural and man-made,
conspire to end the fragile flight,
repeated for thousands of years,
by innocent avian flocks,
assaulted by man
in migration
and in the habitat.

Out Of Thy Dark Hand

L.K., where gone?

That friend I had
I lost to death
who never pausing to explain
moved on.
And the fervor that gave him breath,
empowering the young hunger,
dreaming of a better life,
vanished with a distant traveler
into another land.

Never meeting him again
that flashing smile of exuberant nights
become remote.
Yet sometimes,
catacombs of thought,
sudden collisions with the past,
a stranger met for a moment,
who touched my soul
a distant life ago,
stir the silent tomb
unmarked
on which I sit,
making me dream of some small plot of earth
where lies a friend.

By Gary Beck

Novels

Extreme Change
Acts of Defiance
Flawed Connections
Call to Valor
Sudden Conflicts
Crumbling Ramparts
Flare Up
Raise High the Walls
Still Defiant
State of Rage
Wave Length
Protective Agency
Obsess
Still Obsessed

Poetry

Expectations
Days of Destruction
Dawn in Cities
Assault on Nature
Songs of a Clerk
Civilized Ways
Conditioned Response
Displays
Perceptions
Fault Lines
Tremors
Virtual Living
Perturbations
Blossoms of Decay
Rude Awakenings
Blunt Force
Remission of Order
Contusions
Transitions
Earth Links
Mortal Coil
Desperate Seeker
Too Harsh For Pastels
Temporal Dreams
Severance
Redemption Value
Fractional Disorder
Disruptions
Ignition Point
Learning Curve
Resonance
Turbulence
Lacerations
State of the Union
Purpose
Double Envelopment
Unillumined
Unveilings
Discoveries

Play Collections

The Big Match and other one act plays
Collected Plays of Gary Beck Volume I
Plays of Aristophanes translated then directed by Gary Beck
Collected Plays of Gary Beck Volume II
Four Plays of Moliere translated then directed by Gary Beck
Collected Plays of Gary Beck Volume III

Short Story Collections

A Glimpse of Youth and other stories
Now I Accuse and other stories
Dogs Don't Send Flowers and other stories
Judgments and other stories

Essays

Collected Essays of Gary Beck

www.ingramcontent.com/pod-product-compliance
Lightning Source LLC
LaVergne TN
LVHW041134150826
845673LV00007B/2323

* 9 7 8 8 1 1 9 2 2 8 5 2 2 *